Happiness | Opportunities | Wellb

THE KNOW HOW ESSENTIALS

Your tool kit to support your Happiness, Opportunities and Wellbeing

Name ....

Class ....

School ....

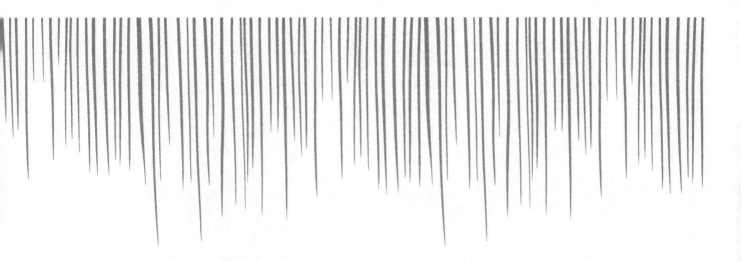

Welcome to...

the KNOW HOW

Being in Year 6 and going to secondary school is amazing, but can sometimes be a little tricky to navigate.

This workbook is full of exercises that you can do alongside our online course in your classroom which we hope will help you find your way.

Just remember, there is no right or wrong, just learning and growing at your own speed in your own way as the wonderful humans you are.

THE **HOW** PEOPLE

Today will be a GREAT Day

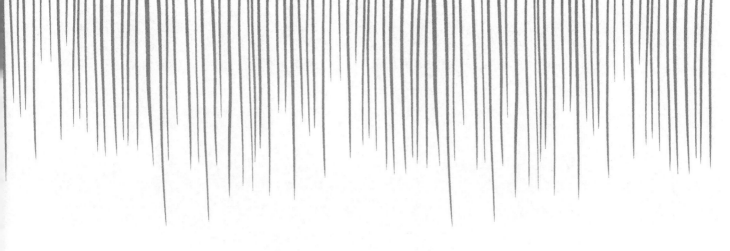

Contents

Bring it on!

Use the space below to jot down all the best things you have done this year, or the things you are looking forward to the most. Remember the joy and get excited for the future.

JANUARY	FEBRUARY	MARCH	APRIL

MAY	JUNE	JULY	AUGUST

SEPTEMBER	OCTOBER	NOVEMBER	DECEMBER

How to develop good habits and navigate social media in the first year of having a phone

'SMART PHONE SAVVY'

5 steps to...

Becoming social savvy

⚡ If things are getting too much, take control of your scroll

⚡ Remember: Screenshot. Share. Help.

⚡ Limit your screen time

⚡ Remove your phone from your room at night

⚡ Be aware of who can see what on your social media pages

If you need to talk to someone confidentially about anything that is concerning you, you can call Childline 0800 1111 or speak to a trusted adult

#SmartphoneSavvy

Best & Worst things about social Media

3 phone habits I have:

my online image in 3 words

I am going to improve my habits by...

2 week check in - How is it going?

HOW would you help?

You're trying to get on with homework and your classmates keep posting annoying messages in the class chat. You don't want to be called a nerd but you need to concentrate.

You find out that some of your friends have a chat that you aren't in. You feel hurt by this but don't want them to know that you're upset.

You posted a photo on Instagram and have received some comments that you look fat and ugly. You replied to these telling them to stop but the comments have got worse.

My advice would be to...

My advice would be to...

My advice would be to...

Use the space below to write down something you have experienced on social media that you would like some advice on. Only your teacher will see this.

Show us who you really are on our awesome social media site

HOWBook

Get creative, and draw your profile picture...

Profile Picture

Name

Describe yourself in 3 words

Interests

Funniest moment

Best thing that's ever happened to you

Where do you see yourself in 20 years?

Proudest moment

TikTok challenge plan

Use this space to plan your tiktok video

Tip: Get to the point

Tip: Prepare and practise

Tip: Keep it short and snappy

Tip: Be creative

◬ ◬ ◬ ◬ ◬ ◬ ◬ Our tech contract ◬ ◬ ◬ ◬ ◬ ◬ ◬

I .... (your name) and .... (your parent/guardian's name)
have decided on the following terms of agreement for smartphone/tablet use in our household.

List terms of agreement below:

....

....

....

....

....

....

....

....

....

....

Notes:

To be discussed next time:

Your Name: ....   Date: ....

Parent / Guardian Name: ....   Date: ....

It's time to get creative! Go with the flow, colour me in, doodle on me, do what makes you happy...

THE **HOW** PEOPLE

DIGITAL DETOX VOUCHER

Cut them out, hand them out, and fall in love with phone free freedom

---

THE **HOW** PEOPLE

This entitles the holder to demand 30 minutes of screen free time at a time of their choosing

*Valid at any time and applies to the whole household or friendship group

DIGITAL DETOX VOUCHER

THE **HOW** PEOPLE

This entitles the holder to demand 30 minutes of screen free time at a time of their choosing

*Valid at any time and applies to the whole household or friendship group

DIGITAL DETOX VOUCHER

THE **HOW** PEOPLE

This entitles the holder to demand 30 minutes of screen free time at a time of their choosing

*Valid at any time and applies to the whole household or friendship group

DIGITAL DETOX VOUCHER

THE **HOW** PEOPLE

This entitles the holder to demand 30 minutes of screen free time at a time of their choosing

*Valid at any time and applies to the whole household or friendship group

DIGITAL DETOX VOUCHER

THE **HOW** PEOPLE

This entitles the holder to demand 30 minutes of screen free time at a time of their choosing

*Valid at any time and applies to the whole household or friendship group

DIGITAL DETOX VOUCHER

THE **HOW** PEOPLE

This entitles the holder to demand 30 minutes of screen free time at a time of their choosing

*Valid at any time and applies to the whole household or friendship group

DIGITAL DETOX VOUCHER

THE **HOW** PEOPLE

This entitles the holder to demand 30 minutes of screen free time at a time of their choosing

*Valid at any time and applies to the whole household or friendship group

DIGITAL DETOX VOUCHER

THE **HOW** PEOPLE

This entitles the holder to demand 30 minutes of screen free time at a time of their choosing

*Valid at any time and applies to the whole household or friendship group

DIGITAL DETOX VOUCHER

WWW.THEHOWPEOPLE.COM | @THEHOWPEOPLE

fuelled by happy thoughts

Use this space to jot down any notes during the session

NOTES

It's time to get creative! Go with the flow, colour me in, doodle on me, do what makes you happy...

YOU CAN DO AMAZING THINGS

Developing your self confidence and learning to love yourself just the way you are

'BEING YOU'

5 steps to...
Realising HOW awesome you are!

⚡ Practise reframing your negative thoughts - remove the 'I am' in sentences. Instead of 'I am rubbish at art' Try, 'I find art tricky but I am working at it'

⚡ Each day reflect back and think about what you have done well

⚡ Be proud of your achievements no matter how big or small

⚡ Thank your body for everything it does for you rather than focusing on what it looks like

⚡ Don't apologise for being you. Everyone is different and we must embrace those differences.

If you need to talk to someone confidentially, you can call Childline 0800 1111
For help with eating disorders call Beat 0808 801 6770 (England) / 0808 801 0433 (Wales)

www.thehowpeople.com | @thehowpeople

This or that?

Circle your favourite option. Be quick. Go with your gut!

CHOCOLATE or SWEETS

CAKE or CRISPS

JAMMY DODGER or CUSTARD CREAM

FOOTBALL or RUGBY

CITY or COUNTRYSIDE

FILMS or GAMING

BROCCOLI or PEAS

ICE CREAM or ICE LOLLY

DOGS or CATS

READING or MUSIC

MORNING or EVENING

SPRING, SUMMER, AUTUMN or WINTER

YOUTUBE or NETFLIX

BEACH or MOUNTAINS

TRAVEL TO THE PAST or TRAVEL TO THE FUTURE

PIZZA or SALAD

SUNSHINE or SNOW

MARMITE or JAM

Shout about your passions, celebrate your talents & embrace the person you are!

www.thehowpeople.com | @thehowpeople

The real me

Instructions: Be honest. Be bold. Be the person you really are.

Shout about your passions, celebrate your talents and embrace the person you are!

What are you really good at?	What is your favourite thing about yourself?	How would you describe yourself in 3 words?
What are the 3 most important things in your life?	What are your hobbies and interests?	Who is your inspiration? And why?
Who is your favourite musician/band?	Write down something your friends may not know about you.	What type of things interest you? Circle as many as you like: Environment Art Crafts Fashion Politics Influencers Food Music Sport Dance Animals Science Home Celebrities Comedians TV & Film
What would you want your superpower to be?	What is your proudest moment?	What would you like to be doing in 10 years time?

www.thehowpeople.com | @thehowpeople

Superpowers

Struggles

Strengths

Change your mind

What I tell myself now	What I should tell myself instead
Example: I am too quiet and I don't think people like spending time with me	Example: Social situations can be quite difficult but I have friends and family who I am more comfortable with

www.thehowpeople.com | @thehowpeople

Guided situation reflection

 Close your eyes and take yourself back to a moment when you weren't very kind to yourself.

What was the situation? Picture it in your mind and try to recall as many details as you can. Where were you? What was happening? Who was with you?

 What did you say to yourself in that situation? What sort of language did you use? What tone did you use?

How did you feel physically and emotionally? Can you feel any tension in your muscles? Are there any emotions coursing through your body?

 What did you do as a result of speaking to yourself like this? How did you feel afterwards?

What could you say to yourself instead? Imagine saying those words to yourself in that tone, in that moment. Do you feel different emotions now? What actions would you take instead in this new situation?

 Does this new imagined situation have a better outcome and most importantly do you feel better about yourself?

My self-esteem journal

MONDAY

Something that I am grateful for is...

TUESDAY

Something that made me smile today was...

WEDNESDAY

Something that I did well today was...

THURSDAY

Something that I did to help someone else was...

FRIDAY

I admired someone else for...

SATURDAY

Today I felt positive about ...

SUNDAY

Something that I feel proud of myself for is...

HOW HEALTHY HABIT TRACKER: CHOOSE A NEW HABIT AND TRACK IT. EG. DRINK WATER, WALK TO SCHOOL

M T W T F S S   M T W T F S S
○ ○ ○ ○ ○ ○ ○   ○ ○ ○ ○ ○ ○ ○
○ ○ ○ ○ ○ ○ ○   ○ ○ ○ ○ ○ ○ ○

Time to reflect

1 thing you love about yourself

2 things you have done for someone else

3 awesome qualities you have

4 things you have done to thank your body and mind

5 things you have done well

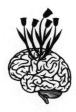 Reflect back on the last week and nurture the flowers in your mind's garden

Use this space to jot down any notes during the session

NOTES

The key to healthy friendships and making new friends in secondary school

'BUILDING FAB FRIENDSHIPS'

5 steps to...
Building fab friendships

⚡ Be clear about what you think is important in a friendship

⚡ Healthy friendships are a two way thing

⚡ Communicate honestly with your friends

⚡ Accept that friendships are likely to change

⚡ Challenge unhealthy behaviour in a friendship

If you need to talk to someone confidentially about anything that's worrying you, you can call. Childline 0800 1111
Speak to a trusted adult if you are worried about a friend

www.thehowpeople.com | @thehowpeople

What's important to you...?

Use the boxes below to list the statements about relationships in order. Most important to least important.

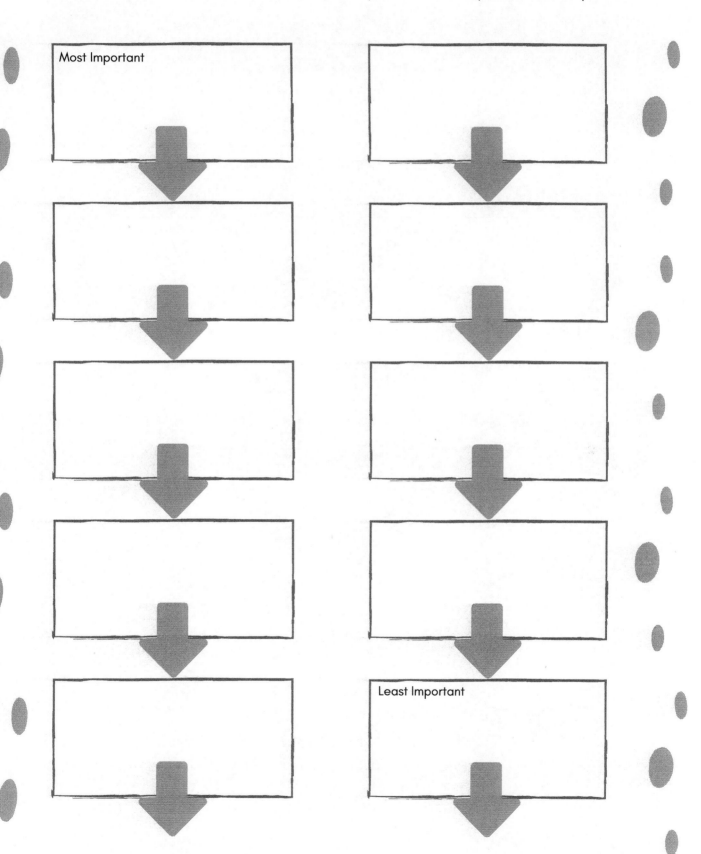

Most Important

Least Important

www.thehowpeople.com | @thehowpeople

Healthy relationship magic ingredients

Everyone finds different things important in a relationship.
Fill in the blank circles with your own ideas about
what makes a relationship healthy.

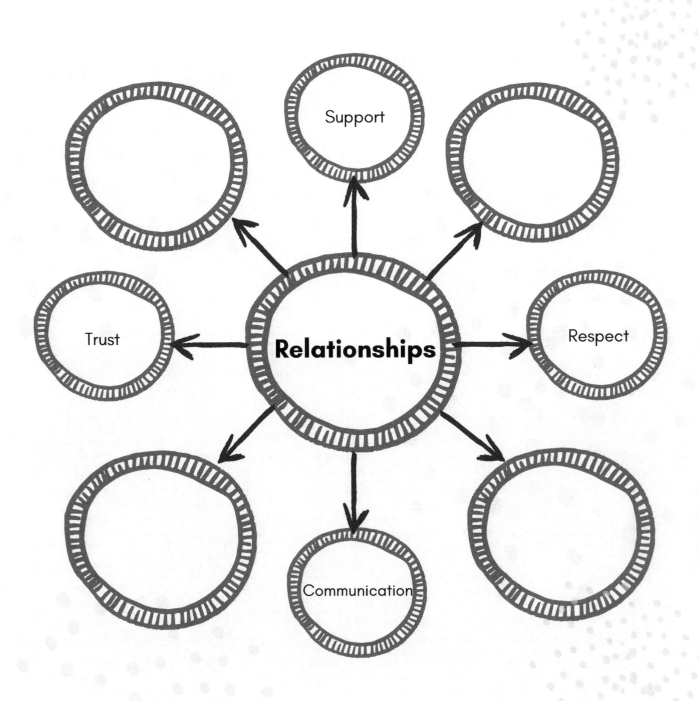

www.thehowpeople.com | @thehowpeople

What would you do?

Are these signs of an unhealthy friendship?
What can you do to deal with the situation and improve
the relationship?

 **The Situation**

You told your friend a secret about who you fancy and you find out they have told one of your other friends.

Your Ideas

Your Ideas

2 **The Situation**

A friend of yours has started to be quite nasty about another person in your friendship group. They tell you that you shouldn't invite them to your upcoming party.

3 **The Situation**

You spend your lunchtime playing football with a group of people you don't normally hang around with. Your best friend tells you that tomorrow you have to spend break with them.

Your Ideas

www.thehowpeople.com | @thehowpeople

My friend promise

What promises will you make to be a better friend and create healthier relationships?

I promise to...

☆ **Creating healthy relationships works both ways.**

I promise to...

☆ **What makes a great friend?**

☆ **What are the most important things to you?**

I promise to...

I promise to...

☆ **Make sure you are doing what you can to have positive friendships.**

www.thehowpeople.com | @thehowpeople

Kindness is Beautiful

Use this space to jot down any notes during the session

N O T E S

The importance of living a life packed full of kindness and positivity

'KIND TO YOU, KIND TO ALL'

5 steps to...

Kindness and positivity

⚡ Be kind in your words, actions and attitudes

⚡ Try to do a kind act everyday

⚡ Being kind to yourself is just as important

⚡ It's ok to feel less positive sometimes

⚡ A smile goes a long way!

Try using meditation exercises and apps such as Headspace/Calm/Stop.Breathe.
Think/Smiling Mind to help you feel more positive.

If you need to talk to someone confidentially about anything that is concerning you or
if you are experiencing unkindness, you can call Childline 0800 1111 or speak to a
trusted adult.

www.thehowpeople.com | @thehowpeople

A kindness a day... Keeps negativity at bay!

Can you be the first to do all of these kind acts?

Tell your family why you love them	Tell someone they are awesome!	Hold the door open for someone	Tidy your bedroom without being asked	Make a home made gift for someone	Make positivity pebbles	Love your world. Plant something
Help nature. Feed the birds	Smile at someone	Bake someone a cake	Help the planet. Do a litter pick	Tell your friends why they are amazing	Teach somebody something new	Chalk a positive note on a pavement
Give someone a proper big hug	Send a positivity postcard	Offer to wash the dishes	Leave a nice note on the bathroom mirror	Give someone a compliment	Offer to help make dinner	Donate to your local foodbank

What other kind things did you do?

www.thehowpeople.com | @thehowpeople

"I am"

Fill in the blank spaces with more positive statements and look at this every time you need a reminder of how great you are!

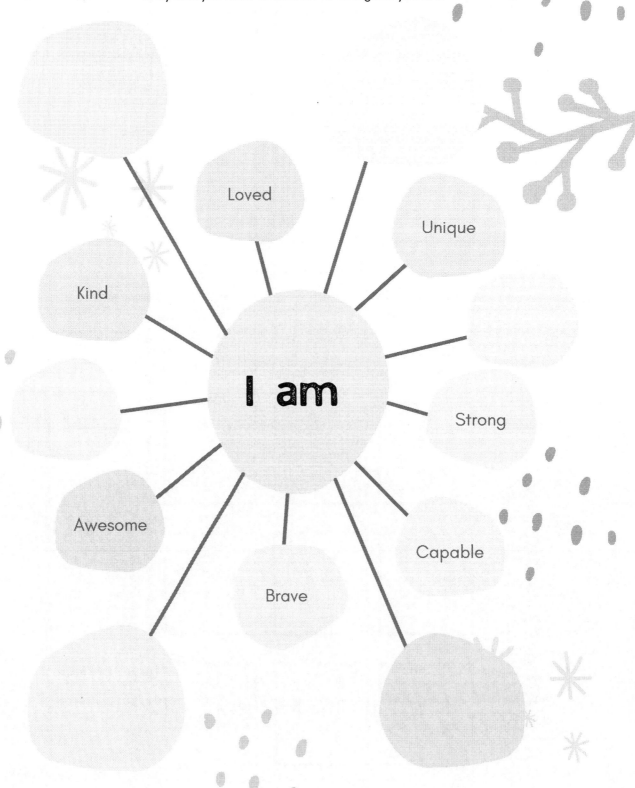

Loved

Unique

Kind

I am

Strong

Awesome

Capable

Brave

Today, I feel...

On a scale of 1-10 write down how strongly you feel each emotion each day.
*Add your own 2 emotions in the blank spaces.

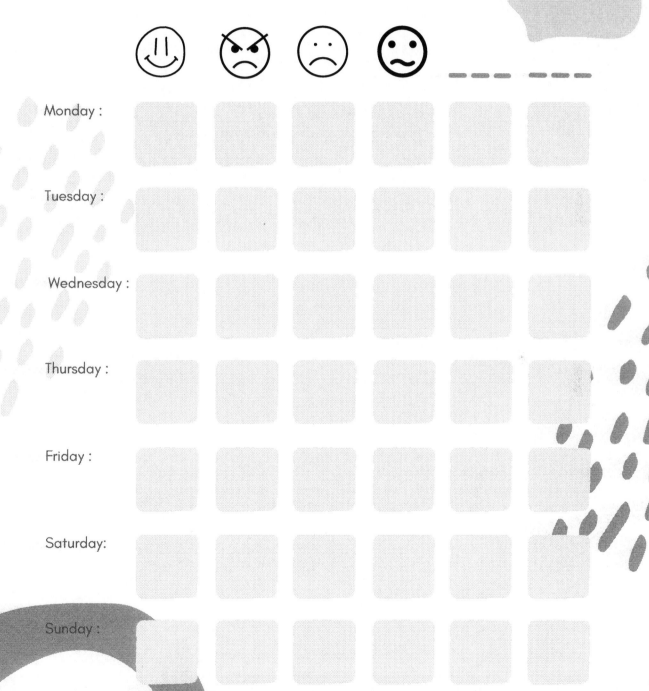

Monday :

Tuesday :

Wednesday :

Thursday :

Friday :

Saturday:

Sunday :

I'm grateful for...

Focusing on the things we are grateful for makes us feel more positive

Use this space to jot down any notes during the session

N O T E S

It's time to get creative! Go with the flow, colour me in, doodle on me, do what makes you happy...

BE THE BEST VERSION OF YOURSELF

NEVER

GIVE

UP

ON

YOUR

DREAMS

Use this space to jot down any notes during the session

N O T E S

Use this space to jot down any notes during the session

N O T E S

Printed in Great Britain
by Amazon